Men-at-Arms • 549

The Dacians and Getae at War

4th Century BC–2nd Century AD

Andrei Pogacias • Illustrated by Catalin Draghici

Series editors: Martin Windrow & Nick Reynolds

OSPREY PUBLISHING
Bloomsbury Publishing Plc
Kemp House, Chawley Park, Cumnor Hill, Oxford OX2 9PH, UK
29 Earlsfort Terrace, Dublin 2, Ireland
1385 Broadway, 5th Floor, New York, NY 10018, USA
E-mail: info@ospreypublishing.com
www.ospreypublishing.com

OSPREY is a trademark of Osprey Publishing Ltd

First published in Great Britain in 2023

© Osprey Publishing Ltd, 2023

A catalogue record for this book is available from the British Library

ISBN: PB: 9781472854537; eBook: 9781472854520;
ePDF: 9781472854544; XML: 9781472854513

23 24 25 26 27 10 9 8 7 6 5 4 3 2 1

Editor: Martin Windrow
Index by Alan Rutter
Map by Alina Bondrea
Typeset by PDQ Digital Media Solutions, Bungay, UK
Printed in India by Replika Press Private Ltd

MIX
Paper from
responsible sources
FSC® C016779
FSC
www.fsc.org

Osprey Publishing supports the Woodland Trust, the UK's leading woodland
conservation charity.

To find out more about our authors and books, visit
www.ospreypublishing.com. Here you will find extracts, author interviews,
details of forthcoming events, and the option to sign up for our newsletter.

Dedication

This book is a homage to our ancestors, who were for many years the
arch-enemies of Rome.

Acknowledgements

Photographs credited to 'MNIR' are courtesy the *Muzeul National de Istorie a
Romaniei* (National Museum of Romanian History, Bucharest), while 'MNUAI'
credits the *Muzeul National al Unirii Alba Iulia* (National Union Museum, Alba
Iulia). The author is also grateful for permission to reproduce photographs by
Radu Oltean and the association Historia Renascita, and to Alina Bondrea for
drawing the map.

TITLE PAGE
For caption to photograph, see page 35.

OPPOSITE
**Copper-alloy (bronze) helmet found at Gostavățu in the
Olt region of southern Romania.[2] Note the two low raised
'combs' from front to back, flanking a hole at the front
centre which suggests that the helmet might originally have
displayed a crest of horsehair or feathers. Two other similar
examples have also been recovered in Romania, and all
three might be either trade goods or captures in war. Many
helmets recovered in the Balkans are variously described by
historians, usually according to their perceived resemblance
to several Greek and Thracian typologies. This example is
described as being of Illyrian type; ancient Illyria roughly
corresponded to modern Albania. (Copyright MNIR)**

THE DACIANS AND GETAE AT WAR

4th Century BC–2nd Century AD

INTRODUCTION

Sources

Two of the most important peoples in ancient south-eastern Europe, the Getae and the Daci inhabited large areas of the Balkans around the lower River Danube (mainly the Getae or Gets), and stretching north of the river into Transylvania (the Daci or Dacians).[1] They were known in their times as fearsome warriors who periodically attacked all their neighbours, and at the turn of the 1st–2nd century AD they became a serious threat to Roman north-eastwards expansion. At one time their rule extended over the territories of modern Romania and parts of Ukraine, Moldova, Hungary, Slovakia and Bulgaria. They were well known to the Greeks and Romans – who encountered them at various times as trading partners, allies, mercenaries, and stubborn enemies – so we owe much of our patchy knowledge about them to ancient writers of the Mediterranean world.

In the middle years of the 1st century BC these two neighbouring peoples seem to have merged into a single kingdom, allegedly speaking a common language; they were ruled initially from a centre of power on the Romanian plain, and later from a fortress in the southern Carpathian mountains of Transylvania. While the ancient sources tell us mostly about their military exploits, literary research and archaeology have revealed some information about their civil society and material culture. This book seeks to present a fairly comprehensive summary of what is known about these peoples, who are considered by many to be the ancestors of the modern Romanians.

While their political entity disappeared from history from the 2nd

---

1   Although the peak period of Getic power preceded that of the Dacians by about a century, the order of words in the title of this book reflects the fact that the Dacians are today the more widely known.

2   Throughout this text we use the term 'copper alloy' for 'bronze' (meaning an alloy of copper and tin), since ancient yellow-metal alloys show many metallurgical variations.

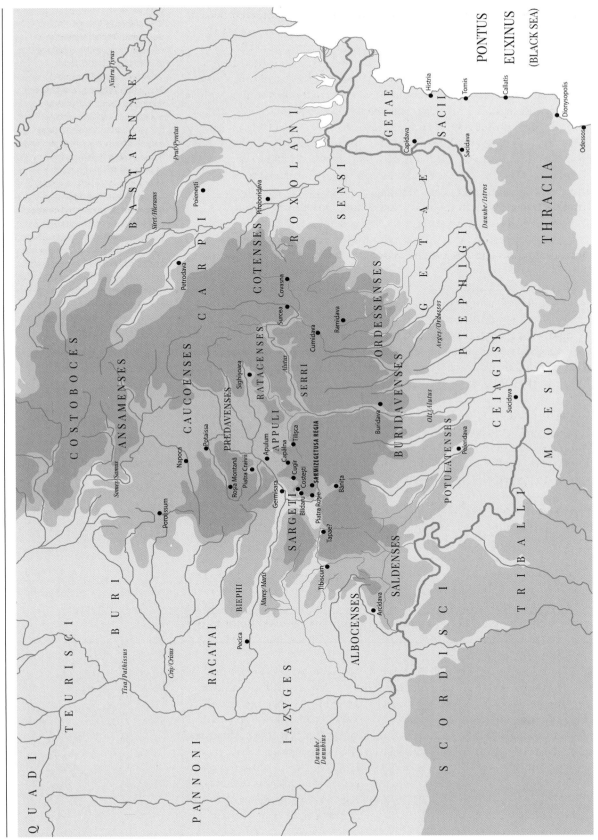

PONTUS
EUXINUS
(BLACK SEA)

THRACIA

GETAE

SACII

SENSI

GETAE

ROXOLANI

PIEPHIGI

CEIAGISI

MOESI

TRIBALLI

SCORDISCI

Histria
Tomis
Callatis
Dionysopolis
Odessos

Capidava
Sacidava

Piroboridava
Poieneşti

BASTARNAE

Nistru/Tyras

Siret/Hierasus

Prut/Pyretus

COSTOBOCES

ANSAMENSES

CARPI

COTENSES

Petrodava

Covasna

Surcea

Cumidava

Ramidava

ORDESSENSES

BURIDAVENSES

Buridava

Arges/Ordessos

Olt/Alutus

Sucidava

Pelendava

POTULATENSES

CAUCOENSES

PREDAVENSES

RATACENSES

SERRI

APPULI

Sighişoara

Alutus

Potaissa

Napoca

Roşia Montană
Piatra Craivii

Apulum
Căpâlna
Cugir
Costeşti
Blidaru
Piatra Roşie

Tilişca

SARMIZEGETUSA REGIA

Bănița

SARGETI

Germisara

Porolissum

Someş/Samus

Tapae?

Tibiscum

SALDENSES

ALBOCENSES

Arcidava

BURI

BIEPHI

RACATAI

IAZYGES

Pecica

Criş/Crisus

Mureş/Maris

Tisa/Pathissus

TEURISCI

QUADI

PANNONI

Danube/Danubius

Danube/Istros

4

century onwards, the memory of its peoples has been preserved both in various surviving fragmentary ancient sources and in diverse works written since then. Drawing upon much earlier writers, whose works were more usually literary than historical in the modern sense, Byzantine chroniclers used the term 'Getae' for the population around the Danube, and 'Daci' for the people of the Transylvanian highlands, regardless of their actual ethnicity. Romanian chroniclers from the medieval and early modern periods, proud that their perceived ancestors had fought the Romans valiantly until eventual defeat by such a formidable enemy, also argued that the country's Latin language proved a partial Roman origin for the Romanian people, who were therefore described as the descendants of the Roman legions and colonists mixing with the Dacians who outlived Trajan's Dacian Wars in the first years of the 2nd century AD.

From the 18th century onwards, and particularly during a romantic 19th-century revival of national consciousness, the Romanians were portrayed in this light, as joint heirs of both the Dacians and the Romans. The Dacians were characterized as the 'good barbarians', who, after subjugation by Rome, adopted the Latin language and entered the wider family of Latin peoples. Nourished by a political agenda, this image supported a claim that the Romanians were the oldest of the peoples living in the region, and that all their later temporary rulers – Hungarians in Transylvania, Ottomans and Russians in Wallachia and Moldavia – were former nomads who arrived much later. Archaeological research also began in the 19th century, in Transylvania by Hungarians and Austrians and in Wallachia and Moldavia by Romanian historians. Artefacts began to emerge from the sites of fortifications and temples, including some treasures – though these were often destroyed by the finders (for their bullion value) before scholars could study them. Ancient writings began to be researched thoroughly, and scientific study of the Getae and Daci started to appear in school textbooks.

Communist propaganda

After the dissolution of the Austro-Hungarian Empire and the Romanian Great Union of 1918, the 20th century saw the rise of a specific historical discipline studying the Getae and Daci, and this was particularly emphasized during the period of communist rule beginning in 1948. The two ancient peoples were presented as pre-eminent in the formation and survival of the Romanian identity, despite centuries of foreign nomadic raids, destruction and occupation. Archaeologists received funds to dig ancient sites in order to recover proofs of the Romanians' local origin and uninterrupted existence.

The communist dictator, Nicolae Ceaușescu, promoted himself as the rightful heir of all the great leaders wielding centralized authority during the nation's history, starting with the glorious ancients: the Getic kings Dromichaetes and Burebista, and the Dacian king Decebalus. (Unsurprisingly, the German Hohenzollern-Sigmaringen dynasty which had ruled from 1866 to 1947 was ignored.) Decebalus was portrayed as a heroic embodiment of the people's strength, courage, endurance, love of freedom and tragic destiny. Imaginatively heroic feature films about the ancient peoples were shown all over the country. State propaganda exhibited large portraits of Ceaușescu in the shadows of these great personalities; songs and poems were taught in schools, sung and recited

OPPOSITE
Map showing the area of Getic and Dacian power in ancient time, wth the names of constituent and some neighbouring tribes (e.g. the Sarmatian Iazyges, west, and Roxolani, east). Placenames are in their ancient forms, but rivers also show modern names where known. Getic and Dacian tribes occupied much of modern Romania and parts of Ukraine, Moldova, Bulgaria, Hungary and Slovakia, where they were bordered by various other peoples of Sarmatian, Celtic or Germanic origin. This map consolidates events over a period of about 400 years, and boundaries naturally varied over time. (Copyright Alina Bondrea)

The carved 'trophies-of-arms' depicting captured weapons and equipment on the base of Trajan's Column in Rome are the main iconographic source for the gear of 1st–2nd century AD Dacian warriors. This detail from the lower left corner of the south-western side shows, among other items, two domed Sarmatian-type helmets with a spike or knob on the apex, and horizontal and vertical banding; decorated elliptical (oval) shields; an unstrung bow and a quiver of arrows; (centre) the decorated head of a *carnyx* trumpet/horn; (top right) a long Celtic-type sword, and below it a tunic with interesting frontal detail, which recurs elsewhere on the Column. (Photo copyright Radu Oltean)

at public gatherings, and rendered as marching songs for military parades. The dictator thus sought ostensibly to legitimize his rule over a terrorized and hungry nation.

Politicized mythology

This communist propaganda also gave rise to an anachronistic trend of thought partially based on some pseudo-historical works from the 19th-century romantic period. The so-called *dacomani* ('Dacian maniacs') are comparable to a religious cult, and perpetrate many lies and inventions. Their main illusions are that the two peoples were always one and the same – the Daco-Getae; that they originally came from Troy; and that they spoke Latin *before* the Romans. The most deluded pretend that the Daco-Getae were the primordial people of world civilization, the inventors of everything from the wheel to the pyramids, and the originators of language and writing, religion, arithmetic and science (and holographic tunnels with teleportation stations throughout the entire region). According to the cultists, knowledge of this civilization disappeared because it was (and still is) forced into oblivion by a universal conspiracy. (While at first sight quite amusing, this deranged movement, deaf to all historical evidence, persists; it is backed by various public figures, some of them former high-ranking communist officers, and attracts generous funding.)

Recent research

On the other hand, over the past few decades interest in Dacian (alongside Roman) historical re-enactment and 'experimental archaeology' has steadily developed in Romania alongside conventional historical study.

The best of these groups are carrying out evidence-based research regarding the Dacian way of life and material culture. Re-enactment festivals – some of them with international participation – and various other activities place the known facts in front of ever-larger audiences. Parts of this book are based not only on the study of ancient sources, scientific literature and archaeological evidence, but also on the author's and artist's many years of participation in these activities. Serious re-enactors keep up with the information appearing in scientific journals in order to improve their gear, and to transmit this information to the public – especially to youngsters – in an accessible way.

While a general consensus about many aspects of the Getae and Daci has by now emerged, there is obviously a huge amount still to discover, record and analyse. Scholarly opinions are far from unanimous, but this brings to the on-going research both energy and the impulse to question previous assumptions. Meanwhile, remnants of the Dacian civilization can be seen today in Romania, of which a few are UNESCO sites still awaiting funding and better administration. Many artefacts await visitors in the museums, and many more are found every year by archaeologists and detectorists. The search continues for these wild riders who, 2,000 years ago, set forth to plunder and strike fear in ancient south-eastern Europe.

SELECT CHRONOLOGY

513 BC	Persian king Darius I the Great (550–486 BC) campaigns against the Scythians north of the Black Sea. The Getae try to resist the Persian advance but are defeated, and forced to join his campaign.
335 BC	Alexander III the Great of Macedon (356–323 BC) campaigns northwards against the Balkan tribes, and also crosses the Danube against the Getae. He defeats them in open battle, and then captures, plunders and destroys a settlement.
292 BC	Macedonian general and future king Lysimachos (r. 285–281 BC) campaigns against Getic king Dromichaetes. Lysimachos is defeated and taken prisoner, but later negotiates his release.
82 BC	Getic king Burebista (r. 82–44 BC) takes power, from a centre somewhere on the Romanian plain.
60–48 BC	Burebista creates a large unified Getic-Dacian kingdom, defeating many neighbouring peoples. He also dominates the Greek cities on the west coast of the Black Sea, from Olbia (Parutine) in modern Ukraine to Apollonia (Sozopol) in Bulgaria – some by conquest, others by negotiation.
49 BC	During the Roman civil war between G. Julius Caesar and Gn. Pompeius Magnus groups of Getae are hired by Caesar's enemies in the Balkans.
44 BC	Burebista dies in a rebellion or by assassination. Thereafter, dynastic rivalries see power divided among four or five leading regional clans.
31 BC	During the Roman civil war between Octavius (Augustus) Caesar and Marcus Antonius, groups of Getae and Daci offer military services to both sides. Many are captured by Caesarean forces, and pressed into service to fight against the Suebi on the German frontier.

29–27 BC	Roman army commanded by M. Licinius Crassus enters the territory between the Danube and the Black Sea, fighting in what had started as a war between the Getic regional rulers Rholes and Dapyx. Crassus defeats them both, and then besieges Genucla, capital of the Getic ruler Zyraxes. Thereafter, periodic Getic-Dacian raiding into Roman provinces of Moesia and Pannonia continues.
AD 8	The Roman poet Ovid is exiled to Tomis (Constanța) on the Black Sea coast of modern Romania.
AD 85–86	The Roman governor of Moesia, Oppius Sabinus, is killed during a major Dacian attack south of the Danube by war-leader Diurpaneus. Following the latter's victorious return the old king Duras cedes the throne to him, and he is renamed 'Decebalus'.
AD 87	First Roman campaign north of the Danube, led by Cornelius Fuscus. Fuscus is killed, and Legio V Alaudae is virtually destroyed by Decebalus at the first battle of Tapae, which guards a pass into Transylvania near the Dacian fortress of Sarmizegetusa.
AD 88–89	Emperor Domitian reinforces garrison of Moesia, then sends a second expedition into Dacia commanded by the governor, L. Tettius Julianus. Although the Romans are victorious at Tapae and continue to advance, Domitian is distracted by a mutiny in Germania Superior, and by Germanic incursions into Pannonia. Obliged to agree terms with the Dacians, Domitian recognizes Decebalus as a client king of Rome, begins paying him subsidies, and provides military engineers and equipment. Decebalus exploits these to increase his military resources, and continues to plot against Rome.

AD 96	Domitian is assassinated, to be succeeded in 98 by Emperor Trajan.
AD 101–102	Trajan leads his first campaign across the Danube and into Dacia. The Romans are victorious at Tapae and Sarmizegetusa and advance deeply, taking fortresses and capturing many prisoners. As winter approaches Trajan accepts an offered truce and puts his troops into winter quarters. Decebalus soon resumes diplomatic and military provocations.
AD 105–106	Trajan's second campaign. Dacians and allied tribes inflict setbacks in several early actions. After Decebalus violates the terms of a temporary truce, Trajan reinforces his army and advances again. After a final decisive battle near Sarmizegetusa, the city is cut off from supplies and water, and falls. Decebalus flees, and commits suicide on the point of capture, but scattered fighting continues for some time. Huge numbers are enslaved, and massive booty from the Dacian gold and silver mines greatly benefits Rome's economy for generations to come.
	Dacia becomes a province of the Empire, with two legions in permanent garrison, and Dacian auxiliary units are recruited. Rebel Dacians continue to raid periodically, alongside other tribes, but Dacia as a nation steadily fades from history.

THE GETAE AND DACI IN ANCIENT SOURCES

The general scientific consensus is that the Getae and the Daci were both Thracian peoples from the mountainous Balkans north-east of Greece. While we know the approximate area that they inhabited and/or conquered, we have no exact idea of the other populations that lived in this region, whose names were sometimes transposed by ancient writers. What is now Romania was home to various groups of Scythians, Sarmatians, Celts, Germanics, Greeks, and perhaps also archaic populations that did not even speak Indo-European languages. Neither is there any way to guess their numbers. The region was very supportive of life, with a good climate, rich plains well-watered by many rivers, smooth hills, huge forests full of wild game, and steep mountains to provide defensible refuges (and significant deposits of gold, silver and iron). In some areas whole communities, while not large in numbers, could actually live unnoticed. Both the Getae and the Daci were probably Thracian tribes which had moved gradually northwards, and imposed their rule over territories and populations which were originally distinct in ethnicity, language and culture.[3]

The Getae

Not very much is known about the Getae, who were described by ancient authors but who have since been left in obscurity by most other scholars. Their more famous 'cousins', the Dacians, have the reputational advantage of having fought the Romans – and especially the great soldier-emperor Trajan – and thus appear in all relevant works of ancient history. This imbalance in their favour was not the case in ancient times, however.

The Greeks wrote extensively about the Getae, who inhabited the territories in which Greek colonies were planted on the western coast of the Black Sea. The colonists had varying relations with them, ranging from mutually beneficial trade to war. The colonists might enlist Getic rulers as protectors of their cities, inducing them by paying tributes, and perhaps also by the offer of shelter inside their walls in times of danger. On a few occasions the Getae arrived in full force to defend Greek colonists against other Greeks, Scythians or Romans. In times when relations deteriorated the Getae would attack the colonists, but were not equipped to besiege their cities, limiting themselves to destroying the agricultural hinterland, looting and burning down villages and taking slaves, until, sooner or later, more-or-less peaceful relations were resumed. The slaves whom the Getae themselves brought for sale in the Greek cities were obtained through almost incessant tribal warfare.

Fragments of works by various ancient authors who mention the Getae have survived, and an early example is Thucydides (460–400 BC). Writing about the 5th-century Thracian ruler Sitalkes, he briefly mentions (*Histories*, II, 96, 1) the Getae: 'Beyond the Haemus [Mountains] he made a levy of the Getae and of all the tribes lying more towards the Euxine [Black Sea, i.e. to the east] on this side of the Istros [i.e. south of the Danube]. Now the Getae and their neighbours border on the Scythians,

---

3   For descriptions and illustrations of their Thracian forebears, see MAA 360 *The Thracians 700 BC–AD 46.*

and are equipped like them, for they are all horse-archers.'

Many of the ancient sources are poetic or dramatic rather than historical. For example, Strabo (*c*.64 BC–*c*.AD 24), citing the 4th-century BC dramatist Menander, writes (VII, 3, 4) a short monologue for a Get. This is disputed because it describes polygamy in Getic society: 'All the Thracians truly, and especially above all others we Getae (for I myself glory in being descended from this race), are not very chaste… For there is not one among us who marries fewer than ten or eleven wives, and some have twelve or even more. If anyone loses his life who has only married four or five wives, he is lamented by us as unfortunate, and one deprived of the pleasures of Hymen.'

Getic/Dacian distinctions

On the difference between the Gets and Dacians, in another passage (also contested by some Romanian scholars), Strabo writes (VII, 3, 12 (C. 304)): 'There was another division of the territory that has remained from antiquity. Some are called Dacians and others Getians. The Getians are those who lean toward the Pontos [Black Sea] and the east, and the Dacians those in the opposite way [i.e. to the west], toward Germania and the sources of the [Danube]. I think that the Dacians were called the Daans in antiquity, from which the household slave names Getas and Daos prevail among those [slaves who are] in Attika [Greece].'

Strabo also states (VII, 3, 13 (C. 305)) that 'The upper part of the river from near its sources to the cataracts was called the Danuvius, and it goes mostly through the country of the Dacians. The lower portion as far as the Pontos, which passes the Getians, they call the Istros. The Dacians have the same language as the Getians. The Getians, however, are better known to the Hellenes [Greeks] because of the continual migrations that they make to either side of the Istros, and because they are mixed with the Thracians and Mysians.' It is interesting to read that although they allegedly spoke the same language, the Getae and Daci called the Danube by two different names in their respective territories. (The migrations that Strabo mentions might be nomadic, but more probably refer simply to pastoralists moving their herds to better pastures seasonally.)

The first writer to mention the Daci by this exact name in a complete surviving work is none other than Julius Caesar, in his *De Bello Gallico* (VI, 25, 1). He describes the Hercynian Forest, which 'begins in the borders of the Helvetii, the Nemetes, and the Rauraci, and, following the direct line of the River Danube, it extends to the borders of the Daci and the Anartes.' Pliny the Elder (AD 23–79) mentions (*Natural History*, IV, 12, (24)) that the Getae were called Dacians by the Romans, and that the Dacians inhabiting the mountains north of the Danube were suffering from the expansion of the Iazyges (a prominent Sarmatian tribe).

We know from other sources that Dio Chrysostom (*c*.AD 40–115) wrote a *History of the Getae*, which is unfortunately lost. His work would

Sculpted head of a *taraboste* or member of the Dacian elite*,* wearing the distinctive low *pileus* felt cap. Without evidence, many still call this sculpture 'Decebalus'. (Vatican Museum, Rome; photo copyright Radu Oltean)

have been very valuable to modern scholarship; he is known to have visited Dacia in AD 96 and had direct contact with the people and their culture. He must presumably also have drawn upon older works that may be completely unknown to us.

Ovid

One of the most important sources about the Getae are the writings of the Roman poet Ovid (P. Ovidius Naso, 45 BC–*c*.AD 18), who spent his last ten years in exile at Tomis (modern Constanţa), on the Black Sea east of the Danube bend. Although he clearly exaggerates some of the backwardness he encountered there – he was, after all, a member of Rome's artistic elite, trapped in a remote backwater – he leaves us information on Getic warriors, their equipment and tactics, and also their relations with the Greeks and with other barbarians. Although he writes harshly about their barbaric nature, he was clearly also impressed by them; he describes them in poetic terms, painting a picture that cannot be very far from reality:

'No race in the wide world is grimmer than the Getae, yet they have lamented over my misfortunes [i.e. some have shown him sympathy]. Their main activity is plundering, which seems to be a proud *modus vivendi* in the area – 'Countless tribes round about threaten cruel war, thinking it base to live if not by plunder.' When winter rages and icy winds blow, 'With skins and stitched breeches they keep out the evils of the cold; of the whole body only the face is exposed. Often their [long] hair tinkles with hanging ice and their beards glisten white with the mantle of frost.' In another letter he writes: 'If I look upon the men, they are scarce men worthy of the name; they have more of cruel savagery than wolves. They fear not laws; right gives way to force, and justice lies conquered beneath the aggressive sword.'

It is interesting that Ovid mentions a large number of Getae living inside Tomis city – he actually writes that more than half of the houses are occupied by them, though this might be an exaggeration. Still, if it is true that Getae actually lived inside the walls, what were they doing there? Were there barbarians in other Greek towns, and if so, how many, and why? We might surmise that they were members of the local Getic aristocracy who had chosen a safer and more comfortable urban life, with their families and perhaps their retinues. Alternatively, perhaps they were nobles who had lost their positions in Getic tribal society and had taken refuge; might this have been one of the reasons for attacks on the Greek cities? Of course, they would have paid large sums to the town authorities, and might have acted as valuable intermediaries with the various surrounding tribes and rulers. Others might have been embedded emissaries from Getic leaders, or

Head of a Dacian *comatus* or commoner. (Vatican Museum, Rome; photo copyright Radu Oltean)

mercenaries hired by the town, or simply merchants, translators and craftsmen pursuing profit and employment.

Language

Whatever the reason, they had mingled with the Greeks, and Ovid tells us that some had learnt a bit of Greek, but that they spoke no word of Latin (and indeed, laughed at him when he spoke it). This ignorance is unsurprising given that Latin was not yet an official language in the region, and was not yet reinforced by the presence of Roman legions and colonists. Greek would in fact remain the *lingua franca* of the Eastern Empire for many centuries.

Ovid makes the important statement that the Getic language was completely different from Greek or Latin. The Getae may have spoken a Thracian dialect, but the ancient Thracian language was lost long ago, and the few Thracian inscriptions found in the Balkans have not been deciphered. After six years spent among them, Ovid says that he had actually written Latin verse but in the Getic language. If only one of these stanzas had somehow survived until our day, we might finally know how the Getic language sounded. Given the claim that the Dacians spoke the same language, they too must have needed interpreters and translators in their dealings with the Romans.

Religion

We have virtually no data on Getic religious mythology or customs. The Getae must presumably have had a pantheon of gods, of whom one known example was a manifestation of the war god named Mars Gradivus – 'Mars who steps into battle'. It also seems that during thunder and lightning storms the Getae shot arrows at hostile gods in the heavens.

Herodotus writes about a man named Zamolxis, a Getic slave of Pythagoras, the 6th-century BC philosopher and proto-scientist. Supposedly, Zamolxis did well before returning to his own country, where, at banquets, he taught the Getae that fearless warriors could achieve a blessed afterlife. He was eventually revered as a divine teacher, and his cult left a long memory. Many centuries later the Roman Emperor Julian the Apostate (r. AD 361–363) wrote that the ferocious Dacians killed as many enemies as possible, in order to earn reward in the afterlife; they were 'the most warlike race that ever existed, which is due partly to their physical courage, partly to the doctrines that they have adopted from their admired Zamolxis' (*The Caesars*, 22).

According to Herodotus, in uncertain times the Daci made a ritual sacrifice of a chosen warrior, who was given a message to the gods before being thrown onto three spears; if he died he was revered, but if he survived he was deemed unworthy.

Despite our ignorance about religious beliefs and practice, archaeology has identified numerous temples around Dacia, which suggests the social importance of priests. Some fortresses incorporated several temples of common date but of different sizes and designs (some rectangular, some circular), for which there must have been a reason. The carved scenes on Trajan's Column include no character who seems to be filling a priestly role; perhaps they dressed like any other aristocrat, and might even have led troops in battle. It is notable that archaeologists have discovered that after the fall of the Dacian kingdom in AD 106, temples disappear even from far-flung territories inhabited by Dacians, and there is no further visible evidence of organized religion. The whole subject remains a mystery.

SOCIAL STRUCTURES

Getic and Dacian social organization

Neither do we have much information about the social framework of Getic and Dacian life. Their tribes must have had chieftains or kings, priests and war-leaders, at the head of a pyramid of merchants, craftsmen and agricultural peasantry. Early Getic tribal life may have been at least seasonally nomadic, but under the unified Getic-Dacian kingdom created by Burebista in the 1st century BC monarchs ruled from Sarmizegetusa Regia, a formidable Dacian mountain fortress in southern Transylvania.

After Burebista's death in 44 BC, his successor Decaeneos was the high priest, and this dual status may have persisted thereafter. We have no idea if the monarchy was to any degree hereditary, or if all kings were elected by agreement from certain powerful families after proving their prowess in battle. (Some have questioned whether simultaneous status as high priest might have prevented them from marrying and having children, though the above quotation from Strabo suggests that celibacy was a concept foreign to Thracian peoples.) Apart from external wars, kings must have had to be constantly wary of rebellious tribal pretenders to the throne or breakaway leaders, responding to rivalries by military force, financial inducements or matrimonial alliances.

The ancient sources tell us little of the attributes of the Getic and Dacian nobility, so we have to rely on common sense and parallels from comparable cultures in order to paint a logical picture of them. The nobility were the backbone of the armies; they provided the cavalry, inhabited fortified towers and larger fortresses, and must have been responsible for raising and leading fighting men from their territories in time of war. The most important and trusted aristocrats formed a royal council to decide upon domestic and external matters. The nobility could also act as envoys; Trajan's Column presents groups of noblemen surrendering to the emperor, which suggests that many abandoned the resistance led by Decebalus and tried to change sides (as was common in ancient warfare).

Silver *phalera* from the Lupu hoard, 6.1cm (2½ ins) in diameter. It shows a winged woman, her hair tied in tails above her head, and probably represents a deity or some other mythological figure. Her decorated costume of a tunic or bodice worn over a longer dress is evident. (Copyright MNUAI)

The bulk of the Dacian population consisted of the commoners or *comati*, who, as throughout the ancient world, were mainly rural peasants. They lived in hamlets, villages, or larger defended tribal centres *(davae)*, pursuing agriculture, animal husbandry, crafts, and basic local trading. In time of war the ablest men would be levied to fill out the ranks of armies.

While the Getae and Daci certainly took prisoners-of-war for slaves, we have no evidence for a systematic structure of slavery on the classical Greco-Roman model. Slaves seem to have been domestic, and perhaps relatively few in numbers. Some were kept and put to work, while many others were sold on into slavery south of the Danube or to the Greek ports on the Black Sea. Prisoners from rich families who were taken on external raids were ransomed for considerable sums. As in the Mediterranean world, those prisoners who had skills – in crafts, languages or medicine, for example – might find tolerable long-term employment by the monarchy or nobility.

Although the Dacians were split into more than 20 tribes, according to Ptolemy (2nd century AD; *Geographia*, III, 8, 3), their patriarchal society was led by a king and the priests and high nobility, with the ablest of the latter providing the military leadership. (Incidentally, only free men of the elite class – *tarabostes* or *pileati* – were allowed to wear the low, forwards-pointing *pileus* felt cap as a sign of their status.)

Administration

The many tribes (see map, page 4) were historically almost constantly at war with each other, so any attempt to pacify and unify them had proved almost impossible. Nevertheless, from the reign of Burebista in the mid-1st century BC the Getic-Dacian state was not merely a tribal alliance, but a unified kingdom with what seem to have been permanent royal institutions. The nobility must presumably have fulfilled administrative as well as military roles, such as tax-gathering, performing judicial duties, and coordinating collective public works. Perhaps they also provided the priesthood in their territories.

Criton, the Emperor Trajan's doctor during the Dacian Wars, writes that some of the king's courtiers and functionaries were responsible for agriculture, and some for the building and maintenance of fortifications. Since much of the kingdom's wealth came from mineral mining, others must certainly have been entrusted with the management of the gold, silver and iron mines, and also the salt mines that provided a more prosaic but constant resource for trade. The sheer scale of the military works achieved – felling trees, shifting earth, quarrying and transporting stone, and building, in a more-or-less roadless and partly mountainous country – proves the existence of a functioning administration, which presumably drew upon institutionalized forced labour. Ovid mentions royal rights of property over land, which the king could divide between his loyal servants. Perhaps the same applied to a possible royal monopoly over gold or other sources of wealth.

Women

As in the case of the Getae, Dacian women were wives and mothers from a young age, and generally fulfilled the domestic tasks of cooking, child-raising, and domestic horticulture. The women of noble families were

14

privileged and enjoyed advantages, organizing the house slaves rather than doing the tedious chores themselves. No doubt higher-class women wore more elaborate clothing and jewellery. Images of women – perhaps deities – appear on a number of *phalerae*, and on coins, and a number of interesting archaeological finds suggest that some may have been priestesses of certain cults. Many Dacian women are represented on Trajan's Column, and some on the monument at Adamclisi, but always in a passive role. It seems certain that Getic and Dacian women took no part in combat.

Settlements and crafts

The Getae lived on the open plains flanking both banks of the lower Danube and stretching west from the Black Sea coast into the foothills of the lower Carpathians. Some scholars believe that they were semi-nomadic (their tactics and equipment were those of a nomadic people), but they also had settlements on river terraces and in naturally protected locations, with ditches and wooden palisades surrounding mud-brick buildings.

For the highland Dacians, archaeology has shown a variety of dwellings, from small dug-in huts to tribal villages, fortified stone towers, and on up to the so-called 'palaces' of the nobility inside major fortresses. It is today extremely difficult to locate the sites of villages built with perishable organic materials. Only the *davae* and fortresses left visible evidence, although some sites were re-used in the Middle Ages (as, for instance, by the Hungarian kingdom in Transylvania). Aided in recent years by the latest techniques of aerial scanning of wooded terrain, excavations have nevertheless yielded useful archaeological results.

Civilian settlements and workshops were often sited close to fortresses, surrounded by cultivated areas to provide foodstuffs. These included vegetables, the meat of various animals including venison, dairy products, and fish. Medicinal plants were grown locally; wine and olive oil, and perhaps also exotic fruits, were imported from the Greek world, in exchange for slaves, honey, wax, and other products.

Like any other ancient society, the Getae and Daci followed various crafts that provided goods for daily use and also for exchange. Without going into too much detail, archaeological evidence has proved the pursuit of the following crafts: pottery, some of the wares being

Sculpted relief probably made for a building in Trajan's Forum and later repurposed elsewhere. Now preserved in the Capitoline Museum, Rome, it is believed to depict the female personification of Dacia. Note the costume: a headcloth modestly covering the hair, and a long-skirted, long-sleeved dress apparently worn beneath a short separate bodice with vertical decorative pleats or stripes. Note also the shields, the large axe, and the *carnyx*. (Photo copyright Radu Oltean)

distinctive of the Dacians; weaving – in various houses, and perhaps also in specialized workshops that produced clothing and various other textile products; woodworking; masonry; and bone-carving (for fish-hooks, needles, and other artefacts).

Given the country's great mineral wealth, the most important craft by far (we might almost say 'industry') was metal-working. All over Dacia blacksmiths produced iron weapons, domestic and agricultural tools and various other objects in great quantity. At the pinnacle of this craft, skilled gold- and silver-smiths produced marvellous pieces, from helmet ornaments to personal jewellery. Apart from local craftsmen, in times of peace many itinerant specialists came up from the Greco-Roman world, attracted by the rich resources and opportunities in Dacia.

ARMIES

The Getae and the Daci were two of the best-known warrior peoples of ancient Europe. Well-armed and equipped, and strong in numbers, they were well known to the Mediterranean world for their aggressiveness and hardihood, and they were hired at different times as mercenaries both south and east of the Danube. Their raids were swift, bloody, and often devastating. In the mid-1st-century BC period of their maximum expansion the Getic king Burebista led campaigns across all their borders, defeating every enemy. The size and power of the unified Geto-Dacian kingdom that he created was such that Caesar himself considered mounting a campaign against what he recognized as a formidable potential enemy. However, because these two ancient peoples had no written culture, we have to rely on fragmentary Greek and Roman sources in order to recreate a picture of their armies.

Leadership
War-leaders were drawn from the wealthy tribal ruling caste from which the kings themselves were chosen. Monarchs were selected for their proven prowess in war; when a king became unable to fulfil this role, he might be replaced (forcefully or by agreement) with a younger candidate. Kings, in their turn, appointed other nobles of proven skill and (it was hoped) loyalty, to hold various fortresses, maintain military readiness in their territories, and lead armies on campaign.

We can assume that among the families of the warrior nobility, military training for boys began at an early age. At the knees of their elders they would have learned tales of heroes and victories gone by. They would have accompanied their fathers in hunting, where they could learn and exercise the use of the bow and the spear, and would later be trained by and alongside the picked warriors of their fathers' retinues, before eventually being allowed to take part in their first raids. Perhaps, at a certain age, they might have been summoned to join the king's court, to serve in comfort as hostages for their fathers' loyalty (while meanwhile learning the rudiments of politics).

Composition and character
Judging by the writings of Ovid, exiled on the eastern coastal plain, the Getae relied mostly on cavalry to control their extensive lowland

territories. They were dressed and equipped like their neighbours, the Sarmatians, and used spears, bows, swords, knives, and perhaps also axes. We have more information on the later Dacians, due to the Roman sources and the iconography of the monuments upon which they are depicted. Like nearly all ancient armies, those of the Dacians were made up of both cavalry and infantry. We cannot know their relative strengths, but the extent of their overall territory suggests that the cavalry, despite its greater expense, might have been the more important even if not the more numerous.

The cavalry was mainly made up of nobles and their tribal retinues, serving for reward and the chance of plunder. Funerary finds show the panoply of such warriors: in the 4th–3rd centuries BC, fine helmets (though archaeologists have discovered only fragments from later periods); ringmail or scale armour; spears, swords, daggers, arrows (and spurs). Given the widespread military successes of the Getae and Daci, the cavalry must have been a formidable force, shaped by long experience in many tribal wars and cross-border attacks.

The infantry was in great part composed of peasant commoners, but led by noblemen. We might assume that the peasant levies were formed around small cores of full-time fighting men provided by the retinues of the nobility, or even by the royal house. Given the number of tribes and the wealth of the leading families, it is clear that they had the manpower and the means to arm and train such men. Besides these 'professionals', a mass levy could be called up to supply the bulk of the infantry, especially in case of an attack on their territory. Greek iconography from the Classical period shows that historically the peoples of Thrace had a strong tradition of light-infantry skirmishing; such troops would be the easiest to raise in large numbers, and were effective in the mountainous heartland to defend the approaches to fortresses. In a world of endemic conflict, many men would possess basic weapons and know how to use them. In the case of sieges, warriors too old to campaign in the open field could help garrison fortresses, while the civilian population could perform the many labouring tasks demanded by such operations.

The warriors who would face Rome's legions were courageous, bloodthirsty, fearless of death, hungry for rich spoils, and also thoroughly battle-hardened. Against a background of continual tribal conflict and raiding into neighbouring territories, from the 80s AD they had launched mass attacks that thrust deeply into the Roman province to their south. In the course of these campaigns they had wreaked havoc, destroying settlements and capturing much plunder and many slaves. When the Romans retaliated the Dacians destroyed regular units, capturing their standards and killing their most senior officers. When fighting on the defensive, knowledge of the terrain and ambush tactics were not enough on their own; Roman iconography shows heavy Dacian infantry fighting in ranks with polearms. Their record suggests that the Dacians' discipline and tactics must have been superior to those of the crowds of individual

A so-called 'Thracian' curb bit from a horse harness, found in a funerary deposit at Bulbuc, Alba county in Transylvania, and dated to some time between the 2nd century BC and 1st century AD. It measures 20cm long by 14.6cm wide (7¾ x 5²/₃ ins). The ancient curb bit was a brutal instrument of restraint, inflicting pain and injury on the horse's mouth. (Copyright MNUAI)

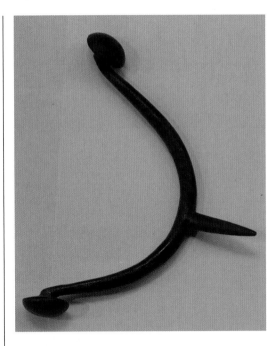

Dacian spur found in a funerary context at Bulbuc, Alba county, Transylvania; it is 6.5cm long by 8.4cm wide (2½ x 3⅓ ins), and it too has been dated to the 2nd century BC–1st century AD. Such spurs have been found in many places in Romania, attesting that cavalry were well represented in Dacian armies. (Copyright MNUAI)

warriors stereotypically associated with, say, the Celtic peoples which they had defeated.

Numbers

It is hard to estimate the numbers in Getic or Dacian armies, because we lack any kind of demographic data. Some Romanian specialists have suggested that the whole population of Dacia around the time of Trajan's wars might have numbered one million people, but this is essentially guesswork. Also, all the numbers given by ancient authors when describing warfare may be assumed to be exaggerations for heightened dramatic effect. For instance, Strabo writes (VII. 3.13) that during the time of Burebista the Dacians could put 200,000 warriors into the field – a number which seems much too high, given that he also states that 50 years later, at the beginning of the 1st century AD, their fighting strength was about 40,000 men.

A clue to Decebalus's strength on the eve of Trajan's wars might be provided by the sheer number of Roman soldiers of all types deployed by that emperor for his campaigns: more than 100,000 legionaries and auxiliaries. The time it took Trajan to achieve final victory (after agreeing several temporary truces) thus allows us to guess that the Dacians had at least 30,000 fighting men (besides a few thousand each of their Sarmatian and Germanic allies), which seems a plausible figure.

Fortifications

The Getae had a number of fortifications, stretching along both north and south banks of the Danube. Some of these were built in naturally defensible locations, such as river terraces, and some were erected over older structures from the Bronze Age. They were made of earthen ramparts and ditches, and encompassed various buildings made from mud brick. Archaeology has produced no complete list of these fortified sites; many were destroyed after capture, some were reconstructed during later periods, and most have been erased by subsequent development.

For the Dacians we have better evidence, since dozens of fortified sites have been discovered and dug by archaeologists. Others have been identified, but in the absence of funding for excavation their locations have not been disclosed, for fear of looting. Dacian fortifications consisted of both so-called 'dwelling-towers', *davae* – fortified civilian settlements – and fortresses of various sizes. Some guarded mountain passes, others were administrative and religious centres, but each had a commander who was answerable to the king. The majority of these fortifications were high in the mountains, or on top of steep hills. It is interesting to note that even the large fortresses did not have interior water sources or reservoirs, which has led some to believe that they were built to resist immediate attacks rather than withstand long sieges. Many were built of stone and timber, using the technique the Romans called *murus dacicus*, especially in the region of the capital, Sarmizegetusa Regia. Some combined stone walls with wooden ramparts, while others had simple ditches and wooden palisades. Some buildings found inside them show that they must have had permanent garrisons, whose families might have lived in a civilian settlement nearby down the slopes.

CAMPAIGNS

There is space here to describe only the most important documented episodes, without seeking to explain in any depth the historical and political backgrounds.

6th century BC
Herodotus writes about Darius's campaign against the Scythians in 513 BC that: 'Before he came to the Ister [Danube] he first subdued the Getae, who pretend to be immortal' [Herodotus later describes the cult of Zamolxis]. 'The Thracians of Salmydessus and of the country above the towns of Apollonia and Mesambria. who are called Cyrmianae and Nipsaei, surrendered themselves unresisting to Darius; but the Getae, who are the bravest and most law-abiding [centrally organized?] of all Thracians, resisted with obstinacy, and were enslaved forthwith…'. The Getae, who believed they could make themselves immortal, were taken into the Persian army and had to take part in the campaign.

Reconstruction of Dacian warriors wielding two-handed *falces*; the weapons themselves are copied from actual finds at Ursici near Sarmizegetusa Regia. Using this weapon demanded speed and agility, and armour was expensive, so these common warriors are unprotected and, in hot weather, bare-chested. (Illustration by Cătălin Drăghici)

4th century BC
The Getae fought other conflicts against the Scythians, Odrysae and Macedonians. In the latter case, Arrian (*Anabasis Alexandri*, I, 3, 5 sqq) writes about Alexander the Great's campaign against the Thracians and Triballi up to the Danube in 335 BC. Seeing the Getae gathered on the north bank of the river, Alexander decided to cross and attack them as well. Arrian writes that they had about 4,000 cavalry and over 10,000 infantry ready for battle. Strangely, the Macedonians' crossing of the Danube was undisturbed by the Getae, so may have been achieved by night. In the morning the Macedonian formations started marching through wheat fields, levelling the crops with their lances (*Anabasis Alexandri*, I, 4, 1 sqq). Light infantrymen led the way, then the cavalry, then the heavy infantry phalanx. The Getae began assembling for battle, while Alexander organized his array. The first attack by the Macedonian cavalry frightened the Getae, who also noted with horror the tight ranks of the phalanx, so they fell back to a nearby settlement. Seeing that the Macedonians were preparing to attack this weak defensive position, the Getae took their wives and children up on their horses and fled as far

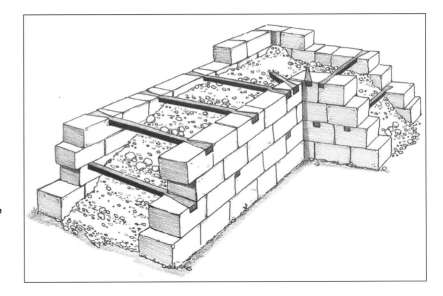

Murus dacicus: reconstruction of the standard method used to build stone-walled Dacian fortifications. It is believed that at the turn of the 1st/2nd centuries AD craftsmen came from the Mediterranean world; in some cases – especially in the area of the Dacian capital, Sarmizegetusa Regia – the dressed limestone blocks show Greek lettering. They were laid without mortar, and some were carved with transverse notches to take wooden beams linking the outer and inner faces, while the space between was filled with rammed earth, clay and rubble. Although the wooden beams rotted over time, the structures endured attacks, bad weather and the passage of many years. (Illustration by Cătălin Drăghici)

as possible. The Macedonians took the settlement, looted it and razed it to the ground, before making sacrifices to their gods and returning to their camp.

3rd century BC

The next Macedonian-Getic conflicts involved the future Macedonian king Lysimachos, who sought to impose his rule over the whole Balkan peninsula after the death of Alexander. The wars between Lysimachos and the Getic king Dromichaetes in around 292 BC are recounted by several ancient writers – Diodorus Siculus, Pausanias, Polybios, Strabo, Trogus Pompeius, Plutarch and Polyaenos. In a first encounter, the 'Thracians' [Getae] had captured Lysimachos' son Agathocles, but, wishing to make peace, they sent him back with gifts.

In a second campaign, Lysimachos himself was taken prisoner by Dromichaetes and taken to his capital, Helis (unidentifiable today, but possibly in modern Bulgaria). A gathering of Getic warriors asked for the Macedonian king to be handed over to them so they could take revenge for their sufferings in this war. In a striking example of the qualified authority of Getic monarchs in the face of a sort of 'military democracy', Dromichaetes had to talk them out of this, arguing that killing Lysimachos would only bring down upon them a more determined successor, while negotiation would bring peace and the return of their territories. They agreed, and a famous feast followed, at which Dromichaetes and his men sat on hay and used wooden plates and drinking horns, while seating the Macedonians on precious rugs and serving them on gold and silver vessels. (It seems doubtful that the Macedonians were taken in by this ostensible play-acting.)

1st century BC

Another episode worth mentioning is a planned alliance between the Getae and the great king of Pontus in modern Anatolia, Mithridates VI Eupator (135–63 BC). The Getae were supposed to attack the Romans in the Balkans, cutting their overland supply routes, while Mithridates was fighting them in Asia Minor. This alliance never in fact functioned.

(continued on page 29)

GETIC WARRIORS, 4th CENTURY BC
1: Getic chieftain
2: Elite cavalryman of a hunting party

1

2

A

DACIAN WARRIORS, 1st CENTURY BC–1st CENTURY AD
1: Chieftain
2: Elite warrior, Transylvania

B

2

1

DACIAN CAVALRY, TRAJAN'S WARS
1: Chieftain
2: Mounted standard-bearer

D

DACIAN WARRIORS, TRAJAN'S WARS
1: Light infantry archer
2: Heavy cavalryman
3: Trumpeter with *carnyx*

BALLISTA CREW, DACIAN FORTRESS, TRAJAN'S WARS
1: Commander
2 & 3: Crewmen

F

DACIAN NOBLEMAN, TRAJAN'S WARS
1: Nobleman with *draco* standard
2: Light and heavy cavalrymen

DACIAN CAVALRYMAN WITH PLUNDER, 1st CENTURY AD

From time to time the Romans would cross the Danube, defeat local rulers and move thousands of Getae south of the river into Roman-controlled territory. This both weakened the northern tribal rulers, and increased the tax yield of the Roman provinces.

In 49 BC, during the Roman civil war between Caesar and Pompey, Cicero (106–43 BC) writes in *Letters to Atticus* (IX, 10, 3) about Getic mercenaries hired by Caesar's enemies. This danger is also mentioned by Virgil (70–19 BC; *Georgics*, II, 495–497), and the poet Lucan (AD 39–65; *Pharsalia*, II, 52–54), who judge that a combined attack by the Dacians and Getae, as allies of Pompey, would have destroyed Rome. Even if they exaggerate, their writings show Roman fear of and respect towards the northern barbarians.

The 4th-century BC Getic hoard from a tumulus at Agighiol in the Dobrudja region of south-eastern Romania. The most striking piece is the 27cm-high (10½-ins) silvered helmet with extensive gilt decoration: apotropaic eyes (i.e. to ward off evil), ears, and on the neck- and cheek-guards figures of heavily armed cavalrymen (compare with the similar example in Plate A1). Note also two non-matching silvered greaves, one with gilt decoration; the smaller pieces include silver vessels, *phalerae* and jewellery. (Copyright MNIR)

In 31 BC, during the war between Caesar's heir Octavius (later Augustus) and Marcus Antonius, we read of Getic mercenaries seeking employment with both sides. Plutarch (AD 46–120; *Parallel Lives*, 63) writes that the Getic king Dicomes had promised significant help to Mark Anthony. Dio Cassius/Cassius Dio (AD 150–235; *Roman History*, LI, 22, 6) recounts that, before the battle of Actium, the Dacians had sent messengers to Octavius offering help. When they received no reply they turned to Mark Anthony, but, being disunited, they proved of no use to him. Many were captured by the Caesareans, and pressed into service against the Suebi on the German frontier.

Dio Cassius also writes (LI, 26, 1) that Marcus Licinius Crassus, Octavius's fellow consul in 30 BC, was campaigning in Moesia in 29–27 BC when he was called upon for aid by a local ruler, Rholes, in what is now southern Dobrudja. This was a period of chaotic internal warfare, from which Crassus duly profited. He attacked and defeated both Rholes's army and that of his enemy Dapyx. The latter withdrew into a nearby fortification; when a treacherous offer to the Romans was discovered the Getae turned against each other, and a massacre followed. Crassus's army then fatally trapped many people who had taken refuge in a huge cave system at Ceiris. Subsequently he marched against all the Getae he could reach, regardless of their original loyalties. He besieged and captured the fortress of Genucla belonging to another local king, Zyraxes, who was absent at the time. Crassus had heard that the fortress housed Roman standards taken by the Bastarnae tribe from Gaius Antonius (a son of Marcus Antonius, and governor of Macedonia in 62–60 BC), whom they had defeated some 30 years earlier.

Suetonius writes (*The Twelve Caesars*, 63) that a generation later, after defeating the Dacians and executing three of their leaders, Augustus, following the death of his daughter Julia's previous husband Marcus Agrippa in 12 BC, 'betrothed Julia... to Cotiso, king of the Getae, at the same time requesting in turn the hand of the king's daughter for himself.'

Gold helmet found at Coțofenești, Prahova county, in the Wallachian region of Romania. Dating from the first half of the 4th century BC, it is 25.5cm high and 20cm in diameter (9¾ x 7¾ ins), and was made from a single sheet of gold; the embossed decoration includes apotropaic eyes on the front and armoured figures on the rigid cheek-guards. It probably belonged to a Getic prince, and the use of this soft metal suggests that it was for ceremonial rather than combat use. (Copyright MNIR)

This must have been during the brief period before Julia's marriage to Tiberius in 11 BC; but the assertion may be only gossip. It seems a very excessive response, even if Cotiso was then conducting powerful raids south of the Danube.

Burebista

The most famous Getic king, Burebista won victories between 60 and 44 BC which altered the geopolitics of south-eastern Europe. From a centre of power somewhere on the Romanian plain, he created a unified Geto-Dacian kingdom which conquered territories stretching from modern Slovakia to the Black Sea (where it dominated the Greek coastal cities, from Ukraine down to Bulgaria) and from the Danube to the northern Carpathians. Strabo writes of him (VII, 3, 11) thus:

> 'Boerebistas [sic], one of the Getae, having taken the command of his tribe, reanimated the men who were disheartened by frequent wars, and raised them to such a degree of training, sobriety, and a habit of obedience to orders, that he established a powerful dominion within a few years, and brought most of the neighbouring states into subjection to the Getae. He at length became formidable even to the Romans, fearlessly crossing the Danube and laying waste to Thrace as far as Macedonia and Illyria; he also subdued the Kelts [sic] who live among the Thracians and Illyrians, and thoroughly annihilated the Boii who were subject to Critasirus, and the Taurisci.

> In order to maintain the obedience of his subjects, he availed himself of the assistance of Decaeneus, a sorcerer, who had travelled in Egypt and who, by predictions he had learnt to draw from certain natural signs, was enabled to assume the character of an oracle, and was almost held in the veneration of a god... As an instance of their implicit obedience, we may relate that they were persuaded to root up their vines and live without wine. However, Boerebistas was murdered in a sedition before the Romans [could send] an army against him.'

RELATIONS WITH ROME
1st century AD: Domitian

Relations between the Dacians and the Romans were not always violent, and there was certainly trading across the Danube in both directions. However, from time to time the Dacians would raid south of the Danube, especially in winter, perhaps when supplies ran low and the river was frozen over. Such was the case in the year AD 85, during the reign of the Emperor Domitian (r. 81–96), when the Dacians mounted a particularly powerful and successful attack southwards into the province of Moesia (roughly, modern Bulgaria).

The much later 6th-century historian Jordanes writes that the Dacians 'through fear of his [Domitian's] avarice, broke the truce they had long observed under other emperors. They laid waste the bank of the Danube, so long held by the Roman Empire, and slew the soldiers and their generals. Oppius Sabinus was then governor of that province... while [Diurpaneus] held command over the Goths [Dacians]... [The Dacians] cut off the head of Oppius Sabinus, and invaded and boldly plundered many military posts and cities belonging to the emperor.' Victory seemed complete, and the plunder must have been enormous in both goods and slaves. Thereafter Diurpaneus was widely acclaimed as a hero, and renamed 'Decebalus'.

Domitian, although not a commander comparable with his father Vespasian or elder brother Titus, reacted decisively. He hurried to Moesia, and his reinforcements managed to put the Dacians to flight, possibly catching up with them as they approached the Danube laden with their spoils. Domitian stationed four legions along the Danube, and intermittent raids and counter-raids probably continued while he prepared to launch a punitive expedition.

This marched north in AD 87, when Cornelius Fuscus, the Prefect of the Praetorian Guard, crossed the Danube on a pontoon bridge. Leading Legio V Alaudae and probably the same number of auxiliary troops – perhaps 10,000 men in all – he headed north towards the Dacian capital, Sarmizegetusa. In this crisis the elderly Dacian king Duras stepped down in favour of Decebalus, whose first act was to send envoys to the Romans offering peace talks. When the offer was refused, he sent another message which was simply insulting.

Roman intelligence about their enemy seems to have been inadequate. A costly and gruesome defeat of the Roman expedition followed at Tapae, a location in Romania which has not yet been identified but which probably guarded a pass into the Transylvanian mountains. Legio V was almost wiped out, Fuscus himself was killed, many Roman standards were lost, and many prisoners became slaves, to be sent as trophies to neighbouring tribes. The fruits of this Dacian victory were immense; Decebalus became even more widely famous, posing an ever-greater threat as he attracted a greater following north of the Danube. Again, Rome was bound to retaliate for this humiliation.

In AD 88, Domitian ordered a second campaign north of the river by L. Tettius Julianus, appointed governor of Moesia that year. The armies met again at Tapae (thus confirming the strategic importance of this location); both sides suffered heavy casualties, but this time the Romans were successful. Julianus continued his advance, but subsequently had to stop and withdraw in the winter, probably because his weakened force was operating at the end of increasingly vulnerable supply lines.

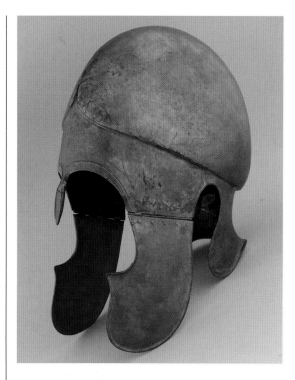

By contrast, this 4th-century BC copper-alloy helmet of Chalkidic typology was definitely intended for battle. It was found in a funerary incineration pit at Făcău, Giurgiu county, in southern Romania. It is 28cm (11 ins) high, with an integral nasal and neck-guard, and hinged cheek-guards. Ancient Chalkida was on the Greek island of Euboeia, and its name recalls copper-mining. (Copyright MNIR)

A simultaneous reason must have been Domitian's distraction in January AD 89 by a military mutiny led by L. Antonius Saturninus, governor of Germania Superior. Other attacks into the province of Pannonia were made by the powerful Germanic Quadi and Marcomanni peoples, who had rejected Domitian's previous request that they attack the Dacians from the west. (Pannonia encompassed, roughly, modern Hungary.)

In AD 89 it was Domitian who was obliged to send envoys to Decebalus, who received generous peace terms; Dacia became a client kingdom, and received money, weapons, war-machines and the services of engineers to build fortifications. (Of course, these specialists also acted as spies, and as intermediaries with local rulers.) While Decebalus had not technically been anointed in person by the emperor, he was officially a *rex sociusque et amicus populi romani* ('allied king and friend of the Roman people'). Client kings were complimented by the raising of statues to them in imperial cities; they could mint their own coinage, and could send their children to Rome for education – while also serving as hostages for their fathers' good behaviour. In return, a client king yielded control of his foreign policy to Rome, and in Dacia's case it seems that some Roman garrisons were established north of the Danube.

2nd century AD: Trajan

Domitian was hated as a tyrant by Rome's senatorial class, who now complained that the Dacian peace terms were shameful, and an unjustifiable drain on Roman funds. After Domitian's assassination by a palace conspiracy in AD 96 he was succeeded for less than two years by an elderly functionary, Nerva, who lived just long enough to name as his own successor the popular and energetic 44-year-old Spanish-born general Trajan – who would go on to expand the Empire to its greatest historical extent.

When Trajan came to the throne in AD 98 the prospects for Decebalus looked bleak, since his status as a client king had to be endorsed by the new emperor. It has been argued by many that the fundamental reason for Trajan's subsequent invasion of Dacia was the wish to capture the rich Dacian gold and silver mines in Transylvania. While this must certainly have been a factor, the truth was more complex. Decebalus had started hostilities against one of the Empire's allies in the region, the Sarmatian Iazyges; he had also sent envoys to Rome's enemies as far afield as Parthia; and he was using Domitian's continuing subsidies to strengthen his fortifications and his army. Rome could hardly stand idle, while this unreliable ruler of a significant regional power prepared to renew hostilities, and meanwhile tied down Roman precautionary forces that were needed elsewhere.

Although historians conventionally describe Trajan's 'first and second Dacian Wars' in AD 101–102 and 105–106, these were in fact two campaigns in a single long war to destroy the Dacian kingdom. It would be one of the hardest wars Rome ever fought, due both to the demands of building infrastructure and maintaining logistics deep into difficult terrain, and to the stubborn ferocity of the enemy. At its peak the army Trajan assembled numbered more than 100, 000 soldiers – perhaps as much as one-third of Rome's entire military might.

Many of the ancient sources for this war are either lost – including, tragically, Trajan's own *De Bello Dacico* – or survive only in various fragments. Still, we can reconstruct a plausible outline of the campaigns and the combatants. The main written source is the 2nd-century historian Dio Cassius (*Roman History*, 6, 1 sqq). Reportedly, by AD 101 the Romans had much better information about both the terrain and the politico-military situation within Dacia; the seconded Roman military specialists, and some pretended 'fugitives from the Empire', had done their spying well, and had even bribed a number of dissatisfied Dacian nobles to abandon Decebalus's cause.

The most important iconographic source is, of course, Trajan's Column, which seems to be a depiction in stone of Trajan's written history. Many scenes are largely generic – soldiers building, marching, fighting, capturing prisoners, and burning down Dacian settlements – but some echo accounts of specific episodes that are to be found among the scant written sources, and some are also supported by archaeology. The monument at Adamclisi in Dobrudja also depicts scenes from what might be the end of the 'Moesian diversion', the famous Dacian raid south and east of the Danube in winter 101/102.

Trajan's Column in Rome. (Lower section.) Scenes LXX and LXXI. In the first, Dacians are being defeated by Roman auxiliary infantry and withdrawing into a timber fort, which is then assaulted by legionaries. (note rectangular shields in *testudo* formation). Many figures on the Column originally had copper-alloy weapons inserted in their carved hands, but these have long disappeared. (Upper section, later in the account). Scenes LXXV and LXXVI. Dacians with outstretchecd arms are asking the Emperor Trajan for peace; Decebalus (centre) is shown sculpted larger. Rectangular standards and two *dracones* can be made out. Right of Decebalus, Dacians (obscured here) are shown demolishing a fortress wall and refugees are on the move with their animals. (Photo copyright Radu Oltean)

AD 101–102

The first campaign started in the spring of 101, when the Romans crossed the Danube on a pontoon bridge and marched towards Sarmizegetusa. After several skirmishes, the first pitched battle occurred once again at Tapae, where the Romans were victorious, although sustaining many losses. The advance continued, with the Romans conquering fortress after fortress and taking many prisoners – some of high rank, including Decebalus's sister. Scenes on the Column show masses of civilians being moved from the area, perhaps even being displaced south of the Danube. Rome's North African auxiliary cavalry attacked the Dacians from a different front to the main corps, and routed the warriors facing them. As winter approached Decebalus asked for a truce, and, since Trajan anticipated attacks from the north by the Dacians' allies the Sarmatian Roxolani, he agreed, and put his army into winter quarters.

Decebalus sought to profit from this, and he may have personally led the so-called 'Moesian diversion', a swift attack south and east of the frozen Danube. The ice proved too thin, and many riders and their horses plunged through it to their deaths. Still, enough managed to cross to attack the depleted garrisons in the area. Trajan was forced to follow the Dacians south with his Praetorian Guard and several cavalry

This shows part of the upper left corner of the south-western side of the base of Trajan's Column. Among the visible trophies are a detailed *draco* standard (note the canine head, presumably representing the Dacian wolf totem; see Plate G). In front of the scale-armour corselet, note an animal-headed *carnyx* crossing what seems to be the handle of a broken two-handed *falx*. At top left and middle right are two domed Sarmatian-type helmets with vertical and horizontal bands and raised decoration; the former shows a hinged cheek-guard, the latter a scale neck-guard. At right are two swords, spearheads and shields, one of the latter with a 'scaled' effect. (Photo copyright Radu Oltean)

detachments, and probably also reinforcements drawn from Dobrudja (Scythia Minor), transported by the Roman Danube fleet as the ice melted. The Romans caught the Dacians and their families and allies in a wagon camp where Adamclisi stands today, in Constanța county. The battle took place at night, and the result was a Roman victory probably followed by a bloody and indiscriminate massacre. Trajan quickly returned to the Dacian front and started assaulting mountain fortresses, in one of which the Romans found the standards and war-machines that had been taken from Fuscus's army in 87.

c.AD 103–104

Decebalus was forced to accept a truce with harsh terms. He had to hand back prisoners, war-machines, specialists, hostages and deserters, and to demolish the walls of his fortresses. Although he was reconfirmed as a client king, he lost huge territories to the Romans – perhaps everything south of the Carpathians – and had to accept a Roman garrison in Sarmizegetusa, probably moving his capital to some other fortified place.

Exploiting what everybody understood could only be a short intermission, the Romans started building a major stone and timber bridge across the Danube at Drobeta (modern Drobeta-Turnu Severin), which was finished in approximately two years. Decebalus again broke the peace terms; he started rebuilding his fortresses and arming his men, attacked the Iazyges, and again sent an envoy to the Parthians. Responding to this news, Trajan returned from Rome. Decebalus tried to negotiate once again, but in vain: the Romans had had enough of his repeatedly broken promises. Moreover, many Dacians had already changed sides, and it seems to have been at about this time that the first Dacian auxiliary cohorts were recruited.

AD 105–106, and aftermath

The exact dates of events are unclear, but it is possible that hostilities had already resumed before Trajan arrived back in the theatre of war. It is claimed that Decebalus made a vain attempt to procure Trajan's assassination. He then captured the commander of a legion and tried to exchange him for peace concessions, but the proud Roman legate committed suicide to prevent this.

The Romans advanced with caution, but still suffered heavy losses while gradually gaining ground. We can only imagine the savagery of the fighting on the part of the Dacians, who had nothing to lose, and wanted to die heroes' deaths to earn immortality. The Romans advanced steadily, led as always by their plentiful auxiliary units, while the Dacians burned down and withdrew from their own settlements; some committed suicide rather than surrender, and some executed their own comrades (as shown on the Column). Probably in summer 106, Legiones II Adiutrix, IV Flavia Felix and part of VI Ferrata, plus their auxiliaries, won a final pitched battle near Sarmizegetusa and successfully laid siege to it. Decebalus himself fled on horseback with a few loyal warriors. He was closely pursued by Roman cavalry, and when he was on the point of being captured by troopers of Ala II Pannoniorum he committed suicide with his *sica* knife. His head and right arm were severed and brought to Trajan. The fighting against small pockets of resistance continued, however, into 107 and perhaps even later. Archaeological evidence shows that the Romans went far beyond the borders of what would now become their province of Dacia, over the Carpathians and to the north and west, destroying major settlements and imposing a new *Pax Romana* in the region.

Writing a few generations later, Dio Cassius described the last Dacian king, Diurpaneus/Decebalus, in admiring terms (*Roman History*, LXVII, 6, 1): 'This man was shrewd in his understanding of warfare and shrewd also in the waging of war; he judged well when to attack and chose the right moment to retreat; he was an expert in ambuscades and a master in pitched battles; and he knew not only how best to follow up a victory, but also how to manage a defeat. Hence he showed himself a worthy antagonist of the Romans for a long time.'

The royal court treasury fell into Roman hands, as later would the immense riches of the country's gold and silver mines. Trajan was acclaimed *imperator* by his troops, and in 107 returned to Rome to enjoy his triumph. He declared public celebrations lasting no fewer than 123 days, during which more than 11,000 animals and 10,000 Dacian slaves allegedly died in the arena. The plunder and the sale of prisoners from this campaign would fund public works which distinguished the later part of Trajan's reign, and would underpin Rome's economy for generations.

Part of the Dacian population left the territory, but others stayed. Auxiliary units were recruited there and sent to neighbouring Pannonia, and also as far off as Britain and Egypt. While merchants no doubt moved to Rome and other cities of the Empire, the local nobility who accepted Roman rule remained to enjoy its privileges. The Romans started building

Detail from the Great Frieze of Trajan depicting his rout of the Dacians, as re-used on the 4th-century AD Arch of Constantine in Rome. It shows an apparently high-ranking Dacian being led as a prisoner by one of his countrymen, both surrounded by soldiers of the Praetorian Guard; at left, one Praetorian is holding up a severed head. (Photo copyright Radu Oltean)

roads and towns and exploiting the natural resources, attracting an influx of colonists from across the whole Roman world. The province thus flourished, and became one of the most thriving in the Empire. Dacian refugees mixed over time with Sarmatian and Germanic tribes to carry out occasional raids, and during the chaotic mid-3rd century Dacia suffered as much turmoil as the other frontier provinces. However, it never rose again as a distinct nation.

APPEARANCE

Sources

The sources for the general appearance of the Getae are slim. Ovid mentions clothing similar to that of the Sarmatians, and their long hair and beards: 'Though upon this coast there is a mixture of Greeks and Getae, it derives more from the scarcely pacified Getae. Greater hordes of Sarmatae and Getae go and come upon their horses along the roads. Among them there is not one who does not bear quiver and bow, and darts yellow with viper's gall. Harsh voices, grim countenances – veritable pictures of Mars; neither hair nor beard trimmed by any hand, right hands not slow to stab and wound with the knife which every barbarian wears fastened at his side' (*Tristia*, V, VII, 11–20).

Other visitors from the Greco-Roman world noted that the locals were rather taller than the Mediterranean peoples. There are clear depictions of their parent Thracian peoples on Classical Greek pottery, and on the walls of Thracian tombs south of the Danube. Typical features include caps of foxskin, cowhide or cloth, with long hanging cheek- and neck-flaps; belted, sleeveless, knee-length tunics, sometimes patterned; long linear- or key-patterned cloaks, fastened by a *fibula*; and knee-length hide boots with flaps hanging from the gartered tops. These images may perhaps be relevant, although scholars have detected more marked Greek influence in the costumes illustrated from the 4th century BC onwards.

For the Dacians we have Trajan's Column in Rome, and the Adamclisi monument in Romania, which is thought to be contemporaneous. The Romans sometimes recycled iconographic features from older to newer buildings, such as bas-reliefs on Constantine's Arch in Rome. A few of eight statues on the Arch, believed to have originally adorned public buildings in Trajan's Forum, may depict Dacians, though others represent various allies including Germanics. Among perhaps 100 other statues of 'barbarians' found across Europe, many depicting Parthians, the detail of some caps being lower and less pointed than the typical 'Phrygian' style hints that they may represent Dacian prisoners – who, although bound, still have a defiant air. Scholars who study Roman iconography dispute the degree to which some costumes may be carefully depicted, while others simply follow artistic conventions. Archaeology is of little help, since finds are limited to metal objects such

Statue of a Dacian, wearing clothing similar to that shown on Trajan's Column. The cloak has a twisted fringe; the tunic, a decorated hem; and the trousers three horizontal lines around the shin, and thongs around the ankles. (Capitoline Museum, Rome; photo copyright Radu Oltean)

as buckles and brooch-pins; the soil in Romania does not preserve organic materials, even in bogs.

Clothing

Taking all the sources together, we can form an idea of Getic and Dacian 'civilian' clothing. Long tunics reached almost to the knee, and were slit at the sides below the waist for ease of movement and riding. Both long- and short-sleeved tunics are shown, sometimes with the latter worn over the former. The materials used were wool, linen or hemp, presumably dyed and set with plant and mineral extracts respectively; alternatively they may sometimes have been woven into colourful geometrical patterns, linear or checkered, or embroidered with decorations. Long, straight trousers resembled the Germanic style, and were tied at the bottom with tapes or thongs. Some ancient Getae in images retain the Thracian boots, but Dacians mostly wear short ankle-boots resembling Roman *calceii*. Tunics were belted, sometimes simply, sometimes with elaborate buckles, and in additional to weapons the belts might support pouches or drinking horns. Large fringed cloaks were used both as 'greatcoats' in cold weather and as blankets when sleeping. We are told that in winter these peoples also wore animal-pelts for protection. The cloth caps worn by noblemen are mentioned above; commoners may have gone bareheaded, but perhaps wore straw hats in high summer. Depending upon their means, men and women alike wore various rings, pendants and bracelets, as found in large numbers by Romanian archaeologists; those of the elite were made in gold and silver.

Women are depicted on the Column and the Adamclisi monument in a rather dignified manner, mostly as prisoners and deportees. (No acts of violence against them are shown in the iconography, but we may doubt if this was actually the case.) It is not very clear if they wear a single long draped dress doubled by a short sleeveless bodice, or if they wear a two-piece costume of a tunic and skirt; they too have buckled belts. Some women wear a sort of shawl over the shoulders. Almost all have their heads covered, a tradition for married women which persists to this day in rural areas. Young women, wearing their hair free or tied in long 'double pony-tails', are seen on various *phalerae* perhaps depicting deities. Some of the women on the above-mentioned monuments are shown barefoot, but Getic and Dacian women certainly had leather shoes.

Belt buckle, 1st century BC–1st century AD, found at Popeşti, Giurgiu county, in southern Romania. Measuring 18.5cm long by a maximum of 6.6cm (7¼ x 2½ ins) , it is made in two layers, copper-alloy over iron, and is decorated with linear patterns and three anthropomorphic figures; compare with Plate B1. (Copyright MNIR)

MILITARY EQUIPMENT AND USE

WEAPONS

Spears and javelins

The main source for the weapons of the Getae and Daci is archaeology. Many artefacts have been found during excavations, more recently by detectorists, or simply by chance (in which case the context is often unknown). They match the iconography, especially that of the 'trophies -of-arms' on Trajan's Column, suggesting that the latter represent items taken to Rome as spoils of war and actually seen by the sculptors who

carved the Column. The monument at Adamclisi also shows various weapons, especially polearms such as billhooks. Experiments by re-enactors, with copies of almost the exact sizes and weights of original finds, have shown how they worked best – especially against Roman troops, both in formation and individually.

The Dacians were masters of blacksmithing, so it is unsurprising that they produced deadly killing-tools. Many smithies have been found by archaeologists all over Dacia, since they are present on almost all excavated sites. Some of the biggest European workshops outside the Greco-Roman world were in Sarmizegetusa Regia. Dio Chrysostom travelled in Dacia in AD 96, and describes what were clearly preparations for war during the Domitian–Trajan interregnum: 'I […] came among men who were not dullards, and yet had no leisure to listen to speeches, but were highly-strung and tense like race-horses at the starting barriers, fretting at the delay and in their excitement and eagerness pawing the ground with their hoofs. There one could see everywhere swords, everywhere corselets, everywhere spears, and the whole place was crowded with horses, with arms, and with armed men' (*Discourses,* XII, 16).

Judging by both the archaeology and the iconography, the primary weapons of the Getae and Daci were the spear, used by cavalry and infantry alike, and the javelin. The spearheads were sturdier, broader and longer, and were attached to a thicker shaft. When it was used from horseback, the spear had to enable the user to break into enemy cavalry or infantry formations, and needed to remain intact for as long as possible. If it broke, or if a close mêlée prevented its effective use, then it was dropped in favour of a secondary weapon such as sword or axe. The iconography shows heavy infantry using spears in tight formations, drawn up in at least two ranks, against cavalry and infantry alike. The perhaps more numerous light-infantry skirmishers were armed with javelins, shorter and lighter with slimmer heads; historically associated with light shields, these could be used in close combat as well as thrown.

The *sica* and the *falx*

Two weapons particularly associated with the Dacians became famous (though both by their Latin names, since we have no idea what they were called by the Dacians).

One was the *sica,* a curved fighting-knife that might vary in length between 25 and 50cm (10–20 ins), with the single sharpened edge along the inside of the curve. Many examples have been found by both archaeologists and modern detectorists, some being particularly finely crafted. Such specimens display decoration on the blade – magical or mythological symbols representing eyes, the wings or heads of birds of prey, or solar motifs – and some have elaborately worked metal hilts. Such weapons were obviously suited for close hand-to-hand combat by any type of fighting man, and the expensive quality of some finds proves their use by the nobility, suggesting that they were a prized symbol of the warrior caste. (The *sica* was also a weapon of the class of gladiator termed a *thrax* or 'Thracian' in the Roman arena.)

The second famous Dacian weapon was the *falx* (plural, *falces*). This term may be applied to any large curved weapon with the cutting edge on the inside. Logically, the Dacian *falx* was probably derived from the scythe, and was developed into a weapon that was deadly in the hands of practised men. Apart from slashing, a hard blow, transmitting concentrated force into the tiny area of the tip, could pierce the upper part of the rectangular legionary shield, whereupon the *falx*-man could pull the shield to tip it forward or wrench it out of the Roman's hand, leaving him vulnerable to another warrior on his left side. Experiments have shown that it can cut through a shield to wound the holder's left arm, although it may get stuck when it reaches the metal boss protecting the hand.

Obviously, the *falx* could also deliver crippling and potentially lethal blows to the head and limbs (and some experiments suggest that it could even damage the classic Roman *lorica segmentata*). There have been a number of significant finds of 1st to 2nd-century AD Roman legionary helmets to which iron cross-braces over the skull had been added retrospectively, and iconography from Trajan's Column seems to prove that this modification was made at the time when legionaries were facing the *falx* in combat. This theory is supported by a clear image from Adamclisi of a legionary wearing such a helmet and thigh-length scale armour, who also has his whole right arm protected by the overlapping iron-strip armour or *manica* more usually associated with gladiators.

The blades of *falces* varied between roughly 50cm and 100cm (20–40 ins) long, and some specimens show decorative symbols similar to those found on the *sica.* There were two versions of the *falx,* without any exact correlation to the length of the blade. One had a short handle, so could be used one-handed with a shield in the other hand, and the second had a longer

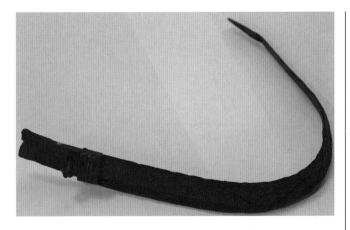

Distorted blade of a *sica* found in a funerary context at Bulbuc; 18cm long by 2.5cm wide, (7 ins x 1 in), it is dated to the 2nd century BC–1st century AD. The bending or 'slighting' of bladed weapons before their ritual deposition is a practice well-known throughout ancient Europe, but archaeology has identified distinct Dacian funerary customs. Warriors were cremated on a funeral pyre complete with their weapons, armour, equipment and various other offerings. After the cremation, bones and metal items that survived the fire were buried in a pit; this explains why many funerary finds are degraded. (Copyright MNUAI)

Falx blade discovered near Sarmizegetusa Regia, as were the majority of known examples of this type of weapon; it measures 42.6cm long by 3cm wide (16¾ x 1¼ ins). Copyright MNIR)

A Celtic-type longsword, probably from the 2nd century BC, found in the Dacian fortress of Piatra Rosie ('Red Stone') in south-western Transylvania. It is 81.9cm long overall (32¼ ins), the blade alone measuring 74.1cm (29 ins). Such discoveries remind us of the influence the neighbouring Celtic peoples had upon the Dacians. (Copyright MNIR)

2nd–1st century BC axe blade found at Sarmizegetusa Regia; at 20.95cm long by 15.5cm wide (8 x 6¼ ins), this is one of the largest examples recovered from the Dacian period. Trajan's Column and other iconography show several axes alongside other military equipment, and their use in combat was presumably widespread. (Copyright MNIR)

two-handed handle; one recovered example of the latter is 90cm (36 ins) long including the complete integral tang for its handle. The first version could be used by an armoured fighter, but the second would only have been practical for a lightly-equipped warrior who could move fast and freely – without armour, the Dacian warrior was a relatively easy opponent for a heavily-armoured legionary.

Famous as this weapon has become, it is notable that, compared to other Dacian weapons, very few *falces* have so far been found. The largest cluster of finds comes from around Sarmizegetusa Regia, leading some scholars to theorize that the weapon might have been associated with a sort of selected 'shock corps' assembled around the capital. A more plausible explanation for their scarcity is either that *falces* were destroyed by the Romans, and/or taken in great numbers to Rome and other imperial cities to be shown off during Trajan's triumphal celebrations; or, most simply, that most were later modified for agricultural use (an easy process), and later rusted away.

Other weapons

The main hand weapon in combat was the sword. The Getae, particularly the cavalry, used long, straight swords similar to those of the Celtic La Tène culture, and these are also clearly depicted on Trajan's Column. However, during Rome's Dacian Wars it seems that the most common were shorter swords of the *gladius* type, much easier to wield for both thrusting and slashing when fighting in close formation. There was also some use of the Germanic *seax*, a straight, single-edged knife with a sharp point. Hand-axes also seem to have been used in close combat, and the iconography shows some axes with long hafts.

Another widely-used weapon also apparently derived from an agricultural tool was a polearm. Archaeology has produced a number of finds, and they are also shown on the monument at Adamclisi. The shaft seems to have been up to 1.7m (5ft 6 ins) long. Some had curved, *falx*-like blades (see Plate C2), but the more usual type resembled a medieval billhook. Their broader blades were between 20cm and 40cm (8 to 16 ins) long, with a pronounced hooked tip, which made this weapon, also, useful against Roman shields, or to cut behind the neck. Alternatively they could be wielded low down by men in the second line of a Dacian formation, to make crippling cuts to the backs of the enemies' knees and ankles. Both two-handed *falces* and billhooks were also effective when protecting the open flanks of a battle-line.

Finally, the Getae and Dacians were also renowned archers, both mounted and on foot, and (see Ovid quotation above) the

Head of a 'billhook' polearm found in Transylvania; 33.5cm long by 4.5cm wide (13¼ x 1¾ ins). Mounted on shafts 1.5m–2m (c.6 ft) long, these were effective weapons against both cavalry and infantry, and could be wielded by men in the second rank of a formation. (Copyright MNUAI)

former were reputed to poison their arrowheads. Trajan's Column shows many Dacian archers, recurved bows and quivers. Light infantry skirmishers might also have used slings.

DEFENSIVE EQUIPMENT
Shields, helmets and body armour

The Column and other representations show shields as large and oval (or more accurately, eliptical) or occasionally round, with a plain or decorated metal boss (*umbo*), and displaying various decorative patterns. Unfortunately no examples or significant fragments have been found, but parallel evidence from Roman finds suggests that they were probably made of wooden strips, fixed side-by-side or possibly overlapped crosswise, covered with fabric or hide, the rims being reinforced either with leather or with metal guttering. We can speculate that as well as wood, some lighter shields might have been made from wickerwork.

Frustratingly, while a number of helmets of various typologies from earlier centuries have been found (see the accompanying photographs), archaeology has yielded only fragments datable to the 1st–2nd century AD. A number of richly decorated (perhaps silvered or gilded?) metal helmets are shown among the trophies carved on the base of Trajan's Column, and a few much simpler ones in the scenes on the Column itself. The trophies may be of 'Phrygian' typology, with a raised, forward-slanting apex, neck-guards and pendant cheek-guards, and embossed decoration (see Plate D1). More common are simpler tall, domed shapes, believed to be Sarmatian. The latter appear to be of *Bandenhelm* type, banded vertically and horizontally, with hinged plate cheek-guards, neck-guards of scale or mail, and often a blunt spike or knob at the apex. (It is notable that while the Dacians' Sarmatian Roxolani allies only appear in two of the 400 scenes on the Column, this type of helmet appears much more frequently in the trophies-of-arms, perhaps suggesting wider Dacian use?) Helmets worn by Dacians in the Column's battle scenes are discernible only with difficulty; some were perhaps made of leather, with or without some metallic reinforcement. It is impossible to tell from this slim evidence what proportion of 1st–2nd century Dacian warriors had helmets. The simplest explanation for their scarcity on the Column may be that only the finest captured examples were taken to Rome, and thus became accessible to the sculptors of the Column.

Barbed, socketed arrowhead dated to the 1st century BC–1st century AD. Measuring 3.65cm (1½ ins) long, it is one of many recovered from the Dacian settlement of Poiana, Galaţi county, in eastern Romania. The widespread use of the bow is confirmed in iconography and by ancient sources, particularly by Ovid. (Copyright MNIR)

41

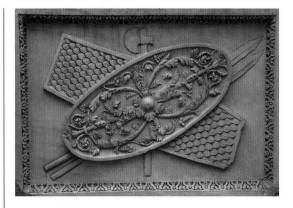

Another carving now in the Capitoline Museum, Rome, also believed to have been recycled from Trajan's Forum. The foreground shield resembles Dacian examples depicted on the Column: large, elliptical, and covered in apparently raised vegetal decoration. Behind it are a long-handled axe, two spears, and a second, apparently hexagonal shield covered with (leather?) scales. Such Germanic-looking shields could have been used either by Dacians or by their tribal allies. (Photo copyright Radu Oltean)

No Dacian appears in any of the battle scenes on the Column wearing any kind of body armour; all, including Decebalus himself, wear everyday clothing. However, once again, armours are represented among the trophies on the Column's pedestal. Some of them appear to be Sarmatian, but they represent a range of types – scale armour with *squamae* of different shapes and sizes, ringmail, and composites of scale and mail; banded segmental armour (of metal or leather), and perhaps also shaped leather cuirasses. Archaeology has also produced many fragments of both scale and mail arrours, and one complete ringmail example. Finds have proved that the Getic elite also used to wear greaves, though there is no clear evidence for the Dacians doing the same.

Finally, given that the Dacians must have taken much battlefield booty after their victories over the legions in the 80s AD, it seems almost certain that a proportion of their warriors would have been wearing Roman equipment and carrying Roman weapons in the wars of a decade later.

Standards and instruments

The Dacians were among the several peoples who used the famous *'draco'* standard, with a decorated textile 'windsock' tail trailing from a metal animal-head mounted on a staff. This seems to have arrived from Central Asia via Persia, brought to Europe by the Dacians' Sarmatian neighbours (and adopted by the later Roman armies from the 3rd century AD). In the case of the Dacians the heads of some of these *dracones* appear to be canine representations of their wolf totem (though one carving thought to be from Trajan's Forum also clearly shows the serpentine form). A few images are found both on the base of the Column and elsewhere, but no such item has (yet) been discovered by Romanian archaeologists. (Once again, it is logical that any captured standards would have been taken to Rome.) The Column also shows rectangular flags, sometimes with fringed or 'dagged' bottom edges; like Roman *signa*, these no doubt bore various emblems or magical symbols.

For coordination in battle the Getae and Dacians used drums, horns and trumpets, including the long *carnyx*. Examples of the latter appear on Trajan's Column and various other stone reliefs, but again no archaeological evidence has yet been found.

TACTICS

From his exile at Tomis, the poet Ovid left us vivid descriptions of the Getic cavalry and their tactics and weapons. The Getae were very skillful riders and horse-archers, specializing in surprise attacks and ambushes. In his writings Ovid keeps returning to the danger that they and their allies the Sarmatians pose towards the Greek cities on the Black Sea. He complains about having (at his age!) to wear helmet and armour and carry weapons to play his part in defending Tomis, despite its locked gates and strong walls. When the Danube freezes over:

'The barbarian enemy with his swift horses rides to the attack...
strong in steeds and in far-flying arrows, [he] lays waste the

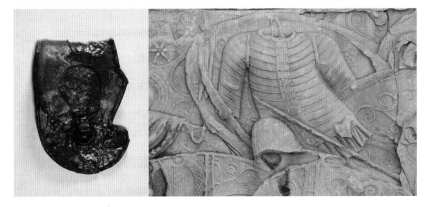

neighbouring [countryside] far and wide. Some [of the inhabitants] flee, and with none to protect their lands their unguarded resources are plundered – the small resources of the country, flocks and creaking carts – all the wealth the poor peasant has. Some are driven, with arms bound behind them, into captivity, gazing back in vain upon their farms and their homes; some fall in agony, pierced with barbed shafts, for there is a stain of poison upon the winged steel. What they cannot carry or lead away [the Getae] destroy, and the hostile flame burns the innocent hovels. Even when peace prevails, there is timorous dread of war…'.

The poisoned arrows are mentioned several times, suggesting that this was a real and feared practice:

'The foe with his bows and with arrows dipped in poison fiercely circles the walls upon his panting steed… to double with a cruel wound the causes of death, [they] smear every dart with viper's gall. Equipped with these, the horseman circles the frightened walls as a wolf runs about the fenced sheep. The light bow, once bent with its horsehair string, remains with its bonds ever unrelaxed [i.e. the Getae carry their composite bows permanently strung]. The roofs bristle with implanted arrows as if shrouded in a veil, and the gate scarce repels attack with [its] sturdy bar… When least expected, like birds, the foe swarms upon us, and when scarce well seen [almost before he can be seen] is already driving off the booty. Often within the walls, when the gates are closed, we gather deadly missiles in the midst of the streets.'

It is clear that the Getae were masters of the hit-and-run tactics of the steppe nomads, attacking the flanks or rearguard of their opponents before wheeling away out of range. We have no reason not to believe that the Dacians did the same, and a few ancient sources suggest this. They mention the Dacians' ability to launch ambushes, charge rapidly, quickly destroy or disorganize their enemy, and then retreat. When defending the approaches to highland fortresses their infantry would ambush

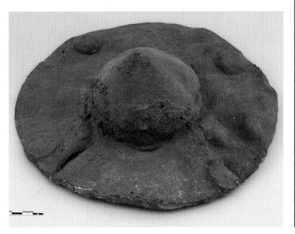

the leading Roman auxiliaries in the thickly forested mountains, perhaps felling trees to block the valley paths with palisades, hurling down rocks and logs or sending burning carts careering down to break the enemy column of march. Such tactics would force the auxiliaries to follow them up-hill into cover, where the Dacians could meet them on equal terms in open-order fighting. While it seems likely that the Dacians would seek to avoid open-field fighting against stronger Roman formations, unless the terrain or some other circumstance offered a particular advantage, it is nevertheless generally assumed that they could fight in close order. They were drawn up in ranks, with the heavy infantry in front with spears and locked shields, a second line with *falces* and polearms, and behind them (having fallen back after the initial skirmishing) the light javelineers and archers. Commanders would stay in the rear, carefully watching the development of the action, while receiving messengers and coordinating their troops by means of flags and the calls of musical instruments.

The cavalry would attack on the flanks, trying to drive off any opposing horsemen and then break into the enemy formation. Before long the opposing infantry battle-fronts would be hampered by a long mound of fallen bodies, and, sooner rather than later, one side had to either force their way over it, bypass it, or withdraw to fight another day. Withdrawal in such a case had to be made in disciplined order, since the enemy would instantly exploit any mistake or sign of panic.

The two parts of a 1st-century BC ringmail armour found in a tumulus at Popești, Giurgiu county, Romania. This example is complete and very well preserved, despite having been burnt on a funeral pyre. It must have belonged to a member of the Dacian warrior elite, since his cremated remains were also buried with knives, rings, a *fibula*, a pendant, and part of a copper-alloy bracelet. (Copyright MNIR)

Large marble slab from the Capitoline Museum in Rome, presumed to have been repurposed from a building originally in Trajan's Forum. It depicts a clearly serpentine *draco,* a short-sleeved tunic with a fringed cloak draped over the shoulders and fastened by a central *fibula,* and part of a spear. (Photo copyright Radu Oltean)

SELECT BIBLIOGRAPHY

Caesar, *The Gallic War* (Harvard University Press; 1958)
Dio Cassius, *Roman History* (London; 1925)
Herodotus, *Histories* (Harvard University Press; 1938)
Horace, *The Odes* (Johns Hopkins University Press; Baltimore, 2008)
Izvoare privind istoria Romîniei, Vols. I & II (Editura Academiei
    Republicii Populare Romîne; Bucharest, 1964 & 1970)
Ovid, *Tristia Ex Ponto* (Harvard University Press; 1939)
Polybius, *Histories* (Harvard University Press; 1979)
Strabo, *Geography* (Cambridge University Press; 2014)
Suetonius, *Lives of the Caesars* (Oxford University Press; 2008)
Thucydides, *History of the Peleponnesian War* (Oxford; Clarendon Press, 1900)

PLATE COMMENTARIES

A: GETIC WARRIORS, 4th CENTURY BC
A1: Getic chieftain
His silvered helmet, with embossed eyes on the front and gilded decorations around the skull and on the cheek-guards, is copied from an example discovered at Peretu in what is believed to have been a princely burial. He wears a copper-alloy Greek-style 'muscled' cuirass (*thorax statos),* from examples found in the Balkans, and on his left leg only a richly decorated greave found at Vratsa, Bulgaria. The long *akinakes* fighting knife, widely used in this region over several centuries, was of Persian origin but copied by the Scythians and Greeks; the extension from the gilded scabbard was used to suspend it from a belt. The rest of his clothing is based on the fresco at Alexandrovo, Bulgaria: a tunic, trousers and cloak patterned in Thracian style, and Thracian boots. In his hand he holds a silver *rhyton* drinking horn with gold decoration, found at Poroina, Mehedinţi county, in south-western Romania.

A2: Elite cavalryman of a hunting party
The copper-alloy pseudo-Attic helmet was found at Găvani, Brăila county, eastern Romania, and is of a style typical in the Balkans at this period. He wears a *lorica squamata* of very small iron scales, with shoulder-pieces and long lappets below the waist, after a specimen found at Malmirovo in Bulgaria. He carries his recurved composite bow, for which the leather case hangs behind his right hip; the quiver for arrows would be slung behind him on the left. He sits his padded saddle without stirrups. The horse's bridle is decorated with silver fittings from the Craiova hoard in Romania, and the long-barred bit is of so-called Thracian type.

B: DACIAN WARRIORS, 1st CENTURY BC–1st CENTURY AD
B1: Chieftain
Note the long hair and beard, as described by Ovid. He wears a fringed cloak over a scale *lorica squamata,* and a belt with a decorated copper-alloy buckle-plate. At his side is a high-quality longsword of Celtic La Tène type, and on his right hip a *sica* found at Bulbuc, Alba county, in Transylvania. At his feet is a gilded and decorated helmet of so-called 'Phrygian' type; this, the scale corselet, and the decoration of both shields on this plate are taken from carvings of trophies on Trajan's Column.

B2: Elite warrior, Transylvania
This figure reconstructs a burial at Singidava/Cugir, where all these metal items were found. He wears a simple round iron helmet with a short integral neck-guard and hinged cheek-guards, and a ringmail corselet. His sidearms are similar to those of B1, and he too has a long spear and an elliptical shield. We have chosen to show Celtic influence in his clothing; some historians have argued that the Cugir burial might have been that of a Celtic warrior who died as a subject ally of the Dacian monarchy.

C: DACIAN WARRIORS, 1st CENTURY BC–1st CENTURY AD
C1: Heavy infantryman with captured Roman equipment
This figure, who might plausibly be identified as a front-rank warrior in a Dacian battle-line, shows at least one Roman item that might either be battlefield booty from the Dacian attack into Moesia in AD 85 or the failed Roman counter-expedition in 87; or, alternatively, from equipment supplied by the Romans under the AD 89 peace settlement. He wears the skull of a helmet (*galea*) of H.R. Robinson's 'Imperial Italic' classification, which has lost its cheek-guards. The ringmail corselet (*lorica hamata*) lacks doubling-pieces over the shoulders, so is more probably not Roman. His primary weapon is a heavy thrusting spear; he carries a hand-axe at his hip, and a strong wooden shield slung on his back. His clothing is a short-sleeved over a log-sleeved tunic, with typical trousers and leather shoes.

C2: Light infantryman
Although its 23cm (9 in) blade is shaped like that of a *falx,* this long polearm in fact qualifies as a 'billhook'. With different blade shapes (e.g. see photo on page 40), these were effective against cavalry, and also seem to have been characteristically used in the second rank of Dacian formations against the enemy's first or even second ranks. They might be used like this, high up to strike at the opponent's shield or neck, or low down below his line of sight, hooking behind to cut his knee or ankle tendons.

D: DACIAN CAVALRY, TRAJAN'S WARS
D1: Chieftain
We reconstruct this heavily-armoured elite warrior facing Roman auxiliary archers as wearing a helmet and corselet both taken from trophy carvings on Trajan's Column. The helmet is of the 'Phrygian' shape seen in south-east Europe, of gilded iron or copper-alloy, with hinged plate cheek-

Detail from the lower left corner of the south-western side of the base of Trajan's Column. It depicts (left) a decorated quiver full of arrows, and (right) a Sarmatian-style helmet, with a knobbed apex. This lacks the nearside cheek-guard, but the pointed shapes of the far cheek-guard and the neck-guard might perhaps suggest ringmail? The skull is decorated with a dagged band above spiral motifs. The shield in the background is decorated with peltate shapes recalling the ancient Thracian light-infantry shield. (Photo copyright Radu Oltean)

Reconstructed equipment of a Dacian nobleman in the period of Trajan's wars. On the large shield with painted decorations is a Sarmatian-type broadsword, typically about 60cm (23½ ins) long, with a characteristic ring pommel, and an iron helmet with copper-alloy decoration and a scale neck-guard. Both these Sarmatian items might have been acquired through war, trade, or the presentation of gifts. Over the ringmail corselet lie a spear, and a belt with a decorated buckle-plate found in the fortress of Ardeu, Hunedoara county. (Photo copyright Historia Renascita, Romania)

guards and a scale neck-guard; it is decorated on the skull and cheek-guards with embossed griffins. The waist belt supports a *sica* knife, and the baldric a scabbard with fine vegetal decoration. The sword is shorter than the Celtic type, and resembles (and might even be) a Roman *gladius;* examples of these with blades up to 59cm (23 ins) long have been recovered elsewhere in Europe. His large elliptical shield is modelled on carvings on Trajan's Column and on various ornamental pieces found in hoards. He appears to be riding a four-horned Roman saddle.

D2: Mounted standard-bearer
Several representations of this shape of standard are shown among Dacian gear on Trajan's Column. The nature of their blazons is still the subject of discussion, but one depicted in Scene XXV bears a symbol similar to a snake. The standard-bearer would have been a nobleman from the close retinue of the chieftain; we show him wearing the low *pileus* felt cap that was apparently peculiar to the upper classes.

E: DACIAN WARRIORS, TRAJAN'S WARS
E1: Light infantry archer
Both ancient sources and Trajan's Column suggest that bows and arrows were one of the main Dacian weapons. This peasant archer is using ambush tactics in broken and wooded country where he needs to move with agility, and has neither the means nor the need to wear defensive equipment. The bows shown on the Column are of the short, powerful recurved type, so probably of composite construction. He would not normally encounter the enemy face-to-face, but would certainly have carried some sort of sidearm – a knife or a hand-axe – for self-defence.

E2: Heavy cavalryman
Although his main weapon must have been the spear, and he carries a sword for close fighting, this rider is depicted shooting arrows at the enemy. His helmet is of a Sarmatian type seen on Trajan's Column: domed, banded both vertically and horizontally, and with attached cheek- and neck-guards. His ringmail corselet allows free movement to use the bow. We show him riding what may be a Roman four-horned saddle, with a leather flask slung at the front; the richly-decorated cylindrical quiver behind his leg is also taken from the Column.

E3: Trumpeter with *carnyx*
This light infantryman has a Roman Mainz-type *gladius* slung at his left side, and is blowing a call on a long and elaborately decorated *carnyx* horn or trumpet. Such instruments appear on the base of Trajan's Column, and on parts of other monuments in Rome associated with victories over the Dacians. Pieces of what may have been a *carnyx* have been found by Romanian archaeologists, but they are too fragmentary for confident identification. The use of musical instruments in battle suggests communications for command and control, and thus a degree of practised tactics.

F: *BALLISTA* CREW, DACIAN FORTRESS, TRAJAN'S WARS
F1: Commander
F2 & 3: Crewmen
We have combined here two images from Trajan's Column: Scene VXVI, showing two Dacians manning a *ballista* on a rampart, and Scene XXV, showing a Dacian fortification with impaled skulls displayed. To these, we have chosen to add a captured standard from Legio V Alaudae, almost wiped out during Fuscus's expedition in AD 87. We know from the sources that the Dacians acquired Roman 'war-machines' and specialist instructors after Decebalus became a client king under the terms of the AD 89 peace treaty, and it is certainly plausible that they had already captured examples during their victory in 87. Pieces of such a *ballista* have been found on the site of a Dacian fortification in a Dacian context predating AD 106. We cannot know the exact appearance of

G: DACIAN NOBLEMAN, TRAJAN'S WARS
G1: Nobleman with *draco* standard
G2: Light and heavy cavalrymen

This leading warrior is waving a 'dragon' standard, with a banded and ribboned tail, copied from the base of Trajan's Column. In this case the head is certainly canine, and, while we know nothing of the Geto-Dacian language, we may perhaps guess that among those peoples it bore instead the name of their totemic beast – the wolf. Originally from Central Asia via Persia, the *draco* seems to have been introduced to the Dacians by their neighbours the Sarmatians; while several are shown on the Column, no such piece has – yet – been discovered in Romania, though one has been found in Germany. It was highly conspicuous, especially among cavalry, with its flutterng fabric 'windsock' tail and ribbons, and ancient sources tell us that when horsemen were galloping the wind blowing through the copper-alloy head made an impressive sound.

The nobleman wears a highly-decorated helmet also copied from trophies on the base of Trajan's Column, and a scale corselet with shoulder-pieces attached on the chest by a Roman-style fastening bar. In the background, cavalrymen await instructions.

H: DACIAN CAVALRYMAN WITH PLUNDER, 1st CENTURY AD

The Dacians were well-known for their raiding across the Danube into the Roman province of Moesia, particularly in winter. We imagine here a Dacian *taraboste* or *pileatus* returning from such a raid with his personal spoils. He carries a spear, and slung from his saddle is his spiked, banded helmet of Sarmatian style, which we copy from Trajan's Column. His second horse carries spare or captured spears, and is loaded with his booty: visible are a Roman helmet, tableware of silver and gold, an amphora (perhaps of wine), and rugs or other textiles, topped off with a large bundle of miscellaneous loot. These objects will either be kept by his family, exchanged or sold. Large raiding parties returning together would carry plunder by the cartload, and drive with them captured animals, and prisoners for use or sale as slaves. These naturally slowed them down, making them vulnerable to pursuit by Roman cavalry before they could re-cross the Danube.

Reconstructions of alternative gear of a Dacian warlord at the turn of the 1st–2nd century AD. The helmet (top) is of the 'Phrygian' style, and the longsword (right) of Celtic type, both as depicted on the base of Trajan's Column. The copper-alloy scale corselet has upper arm-flaps, and the bottom edge shaped in lappets; on its breast is a large apotropaic *phalera* found at Galice in modern Bulgaria, and across it lies a spear with a leaf-shaped head. Laid on the highly decorated shield is a belt with a decorated buckle found at Popești in Giurgiu county, supporting a large *sica* found at Bulbuc, Alba county, and a leather pouch. (Photo copyright Historia Renascita, Romania)

Reconstruction of a fine *sica* with its decorated scabbard. Note corded studs on the silver hilt-strapping, and linear and dot decoration on the double-fullered blade. All the metal parts are copied faithfully from an original find at Corcova in south-western Romania. (Photo copyright Historia Renascita, Romania)

INDEX

Page numbers in **bold** refer to illustrations and their captions.